Separation Anxiety

Separation.
Anxiety

Bradley

Gavin

UNIVERSITY
of ALBERTA
PRESS

Published by

University of Alberta Press
1–16 Rutherford Library South
11204 89 Avenue NW
Edmonton, Alberta, Canada T6G 2J4
Amiskwacîwâskahican | Treaty 6 |
Métis Territory
uap.ualberta.ca

LIBRARY AND ARCHIVES CANADA
CATALOGUING IN PUBLICATION

Title: Separation anxiety / Gavin Bradley.
Names: Bradley, Gavin, author.
Series: Robert Kroetsch series.
Description: Series statement: Robert
    Kroetsch series | Poems.
Identifiers: Canadiana (print) 20210391049 |
    Canadiana (ebook) 20210391057 |
    ISBN 9781772126013 (softcover) |
    ISBN 9781772126129 (PDF)
Classification: LCC PS8603.R33157 S47
    2022 | DDC C811/.6—dc23

First edition, first printing, 2022.
First printed and bound in Canada by
Houghton Boston Printers, Saskatoon,
Saskatchewan.
Copyediting by Kimmy Beach.
Proofreading by Mary Lou Roy.

A volume in the Robert Kroetsch Series.

University of Alberta Press is committed
to protecting our natural environment.
As part of our efforts, this book is printed
on Enviro Paper: it contains 100% post-
consumer recycled fibres and is acid- and
chlorine-free.

University of Alberta Press gratefully
acknowledges the support received for its
publishing program from the Government
of Canada, the Canada Council for the
Arts, and the Government of Alberta
through the Alberta Media Fund.

For my sister and parents: my first readers.
For my grandparents: the first poets I ever heard.

Contents

Hemingway's Cosmonaut

In the sixties, a Russian Cosmonaut fell from space.
I imagine him in a soundless swan dive as below,
Bing Crosby crooned on the Marconi,
and Katharine Hepburn was still playing around with chimpanzees.
Anachronistic, but I never liked John Lennon or Faye Dunaway.
He fell like a lawn dart and burnt up like Sunday morning bacon.
They put his ashes on display in the Kremlin,
next to the reluctantly taxidermied Lenin,
whose stern face seems to say: *tell me about it.*
Then there were these Tibetan monks,
who would wander out onto the slopes peppered with snow
that melted under feet blazing with holy fire,
and mummify themselves, prostrate, for forgotten reasons,
that would only be remembered by Hemingway
who, in the sweet-smelling throes of Cuban rum,
would shoot himself for them, and for all the words he could not touch.
I feel guilty, because I know I would never die for
Tao, or Art, or even the endless Quiet of space.
I might, though, if you asked me to go first,
and see what all the fuss is about.

September

I loved you in the riots.
I found your hand in a writhing barricade of
people stripped down to capricious squalls
of confusion and hate.
Heard your small sighs as the approaching footsteps
echoed off the closed shutters and empty cars
and created ugly music in the blue night
with the cries of mothers and the tincture of shattered glass.
I kissed the small scar on your lip,
illuminated by petrol bombs and angry midnight fires.
Dead children, dead wives, dead fathers
sang in the once-dead blue night,
as I plucked the heathers of your cheap perfume
to lay at the feet of the dead and dying.

Eating Our Words

Peel your husk back, let me swallow your vernacular.
The dirty rhymes you picked up off the stones, or from your granda's lap:
Boys a dear come over here
And give us a while o' yer whist...

How does that end again?
But never mind...
Tonight, we will have a feast of words.

We will dine on patchwork tongues and
shovel down song-stew that sticks
to our ribs and larynges,
like your granny told you chewing gum would,
should you keep gulping it like that.

You'll ruminate for hours, digesting the indulgent cuts
of my half-imagined slang: *guttural Belferstian*;
you can smell the Lagan on my breath,
taste the resin of war murals on my lips.

I will drink your slow, moonshine prairie-drawl until,
throat tingling, belly humming,
you squeeze my arm and carry me to bed,
where I will drunk-dream of child-me
finally executing a cannonball correctly,
into chilled alphabet soup,
and wake up, drowning in diction.

Strange Kettle of Fish

You are a strange kettle of fish,

you tell me,
and if you look closely
I'm sure you can spot rainbow scales
refracting, boiling and bubbling in my Chisen-shoyū-teien,
alongside the perfect Koi,
the venomed spines of puffers and the stony ganoids of a gar.
Even my tongue is rough, barbed with Velcro
and words are pinned in my throat by sharp pharyngeal teeth
so they don't escape when I open my mouth,
and get carried away.

But I can see the goldfish circling and glistening in your ponds,
winking brittle sunlight, momentarily illuminating the low-lying moray eels
lurking in your shallows;
the stingrays and remoras hanging on every word
and shaking with energetic vibrato as I set you on the stove.

Sure,
doesn't the sieve chide the needle for the hole in its tail
and doesn't the pot call the kettle black?

a haon

Although I Can See Him Still—

When Yeats came to Connemara,
searching for the true West of Ireland,
he found it, the true West,
with the drunkards in their taverns,
the fisherman smelling of kelp,
the washerwomen, rough with work and
all of them teeming with life.

When I came to Galway,
for the drunkards and the fisherman and the washerwomen,
I found the body of a dog, a retriever,
left alone on the stony beach.
Its chest was exposed, its jaw unhinged pathetically,
its eyes rolled toward heaven and
its back was broken
across the grey needles of Connemara slate.

That same year,
on the East Coast of America,
we passed a body on the highway,
dignity covered with a thin white sheet,
the ambulance lights flashing noiselessly,
so as to not wake the dead.
Except the body was so large that bits of dignity
protruded from underneath and prompted
outraged blasts of horns from the slowing traffic,
bugling the last post for decency.
In the steak house that night,
people would tear into pieces of dignity,
blue rare, and mop up juices on their lips,
with tiny white sheets.H

I hope they find me as a dead dog.
Supped up by the Atlantic surf and back broken
across the grey needles of Connemara slate,
where even the dead are teeming with life.

Laying the Docks

It became a task for the men and for the boys.
The ones who were still pink-eyed from the night before,
would claim their place in the water first,
half-submerged, backs baking like lizards,
toes curling to find the moon-worn smooth of the pebbles,
and relay instructions:
rivet board to stand, stand to bedrock,
with mystical competence,
and the gravity of astronauts.

The boys, wanting to be men,
would carry the boards too fast;
freckled, sinewy limbs straining for adulthood,
tearing skin on rusted nails,
filling fleshy palms with petty splinters,
and stealing warm sips of beer, with clumsy tact
before tossing them to the approving engineers in the water.
Sure, hadn't they done it themselves, when they were lads?

Sometimes, you would get a board that,
because of the mischievous, crescent-called tides,
would detach, and drift away,
and the youngest of the boys,
would be sent out beyond the shallows,
to where their feet stretched down vainly
like Adam's finger, feeling for the last of the stones,
and have their face stung by a wave.

Then all the older men would
laugh and drink and say
to the boy and his red cheeks
that when he was their age,
he would be happy
to still be tasting the salt.

Brine

My grandfather drank vinegar when he was young,
and buttermilk when he was old.
For everything in between, there was brine.

Gargled over raw tonsils, and poured over fussing heads of matted curls.
Scrubbed democratically over old boot leather, and the good table linen.
Brine was his great leveller; a holy water prescribed for
bloody knees and scraped elbows. *If it stings*, he'd say, *you know it's working.*

To fetch it, he pilgrimaged like Ponce de León to the edge of the Atlantic,
once encountering a Portuguese man o' war
who left him with an Iberian kiss on his heel,
and an improbable tale for his grandchildren.

On winter nights he would take the bucket and
douse the singing turf with his tonic;
a spoor that still makes me think of shortened days,
and the comforting weight of a coal shovel in my hand.

Now, as I fly from old continent to new,
I am glad for the endless brine in between.
Waiting patiently, like him, always ready for my wounds.

Out with the Tide

High crests and low bows,
the wind howl-licks the salt from the sea,
free the load and tie the rigging down;
I am worn sad and thin by the strangeness of me.

The albatross, ageing gulls—
tired-plow a course above the pallid blue,
brief shadow puppets on a benthic floor;
I am worn sad and thin by the strangeness of you.

Rotted boats, splintered oars,
cast soul-empty nets aside,
there is no catch here to be hauled;
I am worn sad and thin by the strangeness of our goodbye.

False Spring

The berries have refrozen,
the bumblebees have disappeared,
the paths are all but covered,
and a pregnant sky cries:
It was a false spring upon our heads.

The beasts are a timid huddle,
their fields are stripped like summer sheets,
they act like ageing emperors,
as a full wind howls:
It was a false spring upon our heads.

The cornucopia is forgotten,
buried under your laughing feet
that trample, with genteel scorn, the rotten summer fruits.
Theirs is the sickly sweet smell of the dead.
It was a false spring upon our heads.

You long for its indifference:
a cold blanket of impassion.
Winter arrives like this, you say.
You and winter arrive like this.

Persephone Starts to Wonder

You send me away with those shoreline glances;
a dismissive wave, an interrupted look, as if,
I was lost at sea,
and you were still searching,
but had forgotten my face somewhere in the long months
with the salty swells, and the blustering gales
removing every line, every imperfect freckle, every crow's foot;
howl by howl.

On the cold shorefront,
(where you used to bury my feet in wet sand,
so that I could be yours for one moment)
you seem to mistake me,
for some rough sea-dog met on a market island,
where tavern doors swell with raucous foreign songs
rolled from tongues sweet with rum
and salted with improbable tales.

You pulled your tapestry apart for me before,
before forgetting my face.
And now the thread rolls between your forefingers,
your calloused thumb,
as you give me those shoreline glances.
And I know my tongue tastes of unfamiliar spices,
and you don't understand my stories anymore.

Blood Warm

Love should not burn, you told me.
Passion should not rage with infernal or angelic heat.
Rather, it should be blood warm, a human temperature;
the functional warmth of a heart.
You taught me that, when,
wrapped in our own affections,
you would cup our hands around the sparks,
blow upon them gently and let them flicker in the hearth.
Knowing that passion is something to be cradled on the chest,
something fragile that your grandmother would place
on the dresser, next to the good china.
A crystal of snow, set still on the tongue,
the moment before it melts.
It exists only in small moments.

Now, those times when you shake me,
when you come to my door, dressed
in your grey funeral suit,
hushing me in grey funeral tones.
Those are the times that I worry.
Those are the times that I think:
perhaps it should burn.
God please let it burn.

Chrysalis

There is no cavern great enough to catch your whispers.
There is no doorway that darkens from your shadow anymore.
No leaves rustle beneath your feet. No field mice are disturbed.
No window panes fog at your delicate breath.

You catch butterflies in a net and let the tired moths away;
their hideousness a key to their cell.
You set out to trap beauty, and you do it well;
there are hundreds of butterflies frozen in glass upon your shelf.

Pockets

There is something small and living,
hidden in your shirt pocket.
I see you whisper to it, soothing words,
when you think no one is around.

My father once told me
that shirt pockets are only for important things,
treasures you want to keep close,
and I think I understand

and wish that you whispered to me like that,
and that I could live in your pocket too.

Why Couples Are Like Expressionists

You learn to pick up the tone from a swirl of patterns:
a dollop of unforeseen mauve, a splash of quarrelsome russet.
Missed beats are sensed by the pricking of a thumb
or a dull pain in your bum leg.
Some hurts have a taste.
Small betrayals have a smell,
and everything, *everything*, has a feel.

So when you ask me, three days later,
why I haven't eaten,
why I haven't slept, again,
I could quicker tell you what disappointment sounds like.

Hidden Moons

The dreams I have to capture life
as a bluebottle under glass,
parade it like a DAR daughter descending
dutifully upon a room
of expectant socialites
smelling of gin,
seem half-formed, and insubstantial;
they disappear
when I forget to look for them,
like a mid-day moon
or the freckles on your neck,
and now, I think
I'd happily take
your hand and realness
over hidden moons and bluebottles.

Mead

Then there are those mead-thick, midnight conversations.
The heady talks, ringing with the song-snap of a juniper berry
breaking away from its twig.
Drunken dream words, thin as hoarfrost on the window,
that turn to uncountable droplets of dew on the morning lawn,
where it will smell of the past night's rain
and the lingering musk of angry sentences
that we might not remember,
but regret, all the same.

a dó

Sanctuary

We are not yet the rough men of the North.
Not yet scornful of the frost, nor canny to the moods of the wind.
Our sanctuaries are built with unlined hands,
and pine splinters in the soft palms,
of merchants, tailors, clerks, trying to ignore the tongues
that still recall the taste of sea salt in a catch,
and the kisses of warm, blushed, country women.

Here, at the end of the world, God is too close.
He does not reside in damp, lit churches,
heavy with people, thick with comfortable mutterings,
but is bound to wild animals,
hunts in sprawling forests, and aches for company in empty tundra.
He is in the blood and the stones and the fire.
We build high walls, in case we should see him.

In some Rue in Paris,
In some Avenue in London,
The women run contented fingers through fine fur,
and gleaming eyes over the envious;
the heavy musk, swallowed by sweet Moroccan scents from nearby
perfumeries.
Here, at the end of the world, we are waiting to forget.
We are waiting to become the rough men of the North.
Somewhere outside, God howls.

Blue Plain Skies

There is too much sky here, too much blue.
Back home, where God retired in the land,
the drowned grass, the rain-soaked trees,
there are holy mountains
that stigmatic saints would fetch up on their knees;
pilgrimages to fill their palms,
bloody their legs,
and save us from getting lost in the tiring blue.
It should be grey.
It should be the colour of weekdays.
Not the colour of aspirations, of romanticized sorrow;
true sorrow is grey, and does not end.

Your God here must pay attention to the advertisements;
red sells men,
purple sells women,
blue traps the lot.

Homebody Ghosts

There are those sweet night thoughts
that broil my slumber,
and shift frozen dreams
to hot, creaking Louisiana shacks,
where they can live warm-cheeked bourbon lives,
among the saltwater vines, and the skeeters;
noonish sleeps interrupted by kind consternations
of a laugh-lined '93 prom queen,
passing screaming tykes from pink arms,
to rest upon a gut, large and full from crawfish and beer.
With tools rusting in the yard,
and tyres sinking contentedly into the swamp,
my dreams are thick, sweet, and smell of smoke.

I awake to the gentle knock of snow at the window,
and a gust of wind beneath the door.

III

God Moves His Divan

Caught in the lightning storm,
I feel for your hand,
and find nothing
but thick sizzling air.

The silence before the strikes petrifies me;
shakes me sure of the existence of wrath.
A panic of the chased hare, heeled by the fox,
courses through me like the terrible volts
I am trying not to think about.
My fear is the addled mind of prey before predator;
the ant beneath the magnifying glass.

I have a small, treacherous thought.
If you were on the other side of town,
and you never knew it was me,
if not even God knew,
would I hand you over
to the astronomical odds,
the spiteful blue forks?
After all,
you're more likely to be eaten
by a great white,
or have your skull caved in
by a Sunday golfer's
mulligan.

Wearing the guilt that makes me
apologize after saying *Jesus Christ*,
like the Turin Shroud,

I make tenuous pacts
with forgotten gods; *Zeus, Taranis, Perun...*
If any of them spare me,
I have a soul, barely used,
I'd cash it in like a pair of car keys
tossed unthinkingly across the money-green felt
on the tables of Monte Carlo or Atlantic City.

I barter with memories of gods, because
I'm sure they won't collect.
In the lightning storm,
I begin to understand the point you made about disingenuousness.

Now, closing the door quiet,
pretending to shiver from the downpour,
you ask: *Did you get caught in the storm?*
It's just God moving His furniture, I laugh
and try not to catch your eye, wondering
what pacts you would have made.

Gossamer

The people here are thin, made of spit-through threads.
But I am gossamer, and less substantial than
the pieces of lint that slow the dryer down
on a Wednesday evening.

Stringless puppets have had more will.
Tsetse flies, with one sycophantic bite have had more influence
with a purple mark on some sub-Saharan décolletage,
than I shall in the forty-some years of life predicted
by a personal cocktail of genetic diseases.
A Manhattan of lung, bone, bowel cancers,
the tiny, paper umbrella of heart disease.
My convictions are as strong as a wasp's wind.
My voice as significant as a gnat's moral indignation.
But,
for you, I could be mountainous.
Catastrophic.
For you I could be a tyrant.
Infinitely cruel, infamously capricious;
a temper unrivalled by Boudica or Cú Chulainn.
Or,
I may deign a distant, icy, benevolence,
receive with scorn, praise and prayers,
assume an aloof omnipotence,
demanding love in frozen cumulus palaces.
Our
terrible power could herald
a wrathful war that shakes ancient giants from slumber and
scorches the earth so that nothing grows again.
There is no destruction that we are not capable of.
There is no soul we couldn't damn.

Or,
I could promise to call you after work,
to let you know I got home safe.
And you could promise to turn the lights off
before falling asleep.

What We Can Learn from Gutenberg and the Protestants

What with the price of ink and the price of paper
being what they are,
new words are at a premium,
not seen since the Reformation
when Gutenberg would hush through the smoky streets
of Strasbourg dressed in morning fog,
and dredge up his press from the Rhine,
in a tanned, dripping, pig-skin bundle
to type a single pamphlet of soap-box litanies
that would get him a nameless grave in a forgotten cemetery;
much worse than scowls from irate shoppers
and the hurt of seeing a head peeking above the sofa
from your perch at their front door.

Now, and here's me a good Catholic boy,
thanking the reformed church,
the death of tithes, predetermination,
Luther and Calvin and even Cromwell,
the only person my grandmother ever called
a bastard, a real honest-to-God bastard;
thank the misplaced bones of Johannes himself,
for the pretty thought that maybe
this doesn't have to be forever;

maybe some things can be lost.

The Fox

A fox moved in beneath our shed, this past Tuesday night.
In the moonlight, he seemed to be covered in black ichor;
a ghoulish dress, a lunar trick.
The morning revealed small, sad speckles of blood,
not his, but I wonder about his age,
and why there is no clever vixen to lick him clean,
no spry kits, to help him break the idiot chicken's neck.
He looks so tired.
He sits under the rotten pine boards and waits for the rain to stop,
like a child crouching with tightly coiled impatience,
under the porch shelter, awaiting permission to play.
He never ventures out to wash the blood from his coat,
and I wonder if his imperfect pelage is important, precious even,
or perhaps just another unimportance in a life,
with no clever vixen to lick him clean,
no spry kits, to help him break the idiot chicken's neck.
Tomorrow night your brother says he'll take the gun
and deal with him, to save the hens, but
the hens don't need much saving,
avian messiahs are in short demand.
They have low aspirations for life,
lower than a fox, at least,
and the part of me that wonders about his stained fur, his age,
and why there is no clever vixen to lick him clean,
no spry kits, to help him break the idiot chicken's neck.

That part of me thinks that nothing should die
tired, alone, and waiting for the rain to stop.

Crossing the River with Hera

Once, when you were an old crone,
I picked you up and carried you across the river.
An antiquated farm-boy gesture
that you loved me for.

On the far bank, your age melted away,
like Icarus' too-cheap wax, or marzipan
in your mother's parlour.

You peered at me with beatific favour;
I had won your sport, affection, youth,
and the other gods would smile on me for it:
Zeus giving his blessing,
Aphrodite withholding her scorn, even
Narcissus would concede that he was impressed.

Now though, as we wade from the shore,
the wind chills my bones,
the cold water shreds my nerves,
and with the same stare, you tell me that gods,
like love and physics: Newtonian, Quantum, Relative,
do not bother with human frailties.

And it doesn't do to believe in Myths these days anyway.

a trí

It'll Be Good for the Kids

Mass was always a grand event as a child, not to be missed.
A whole blessed hour where my parents' attention
was on their mortal souls, and not me;
time for them to be helicoptered by the almighty for a change.

Once, when I was very little, I'm told I escaped,
with the gusto of Steve McQueen gunning it for the barbed wire.
I weaved in between the lines of communion goers,
like *Ski Sunday* on the slopes of Sinai;
the men who were too hungover to receive,
looking up from red-eyed penance to glare.
Their hearts weren't in it though,
they were in enough trouble for the morning.

Finally, dodging spittle from the priest like machine-gun fire,
I laid siege to the altar as if it were Normandy.
With every round missing, the Fr. would aim
with righteous venom at my mother,
who was a bit too young to be having two children anyway,
if he was any judge.

My grandmother, a sommelier of holy men,
feared in seminaries up and down the country,
reserved a truly sacred hatred for a priest
who wouldn't let the children play during the delivery of God's word.
Didn't Christ himself fall from an olive tree when he was a wee'un?

I never have been able to find that passage,
but Bowie said
to let the children boogie,
and he definitely made it across the pond.

Unburst Lights

Bomb scares meant the motorways closed,
and you couldn't get the bus into town.
You'd see mothers hurrying their toddlers' unsure steps,
like they were ushering their husbands from the bar,

and you wouldn't mean to,
but you'd remember
Omagh,
and of course it wouldn't,
but it did mean

a day of tingling limbs and itching palms,
as if your fingers were disappearing fuses,

a night with technicolour whorls in front of your eyes,
as if already blinded by those beautiful unburst lights,
tucked up for the evening with a loving kiss,
in some pram or trolley or a Rover Metro by the city hall.

But they also meant a half-day off school.
Now *there's* an exercise in Catholic guilt
they couldn't teach, with a thousand nuns
and a thousand rosaries.

The Blazer Brigade

Old November Men:
their creaking chairs,
doused in gasoline,
while young upstarts,
noses pressed against the window,
peer in, rubbing gleeful hands together;
hands that glow with fresh, young blood,
muscles and bones that stretch with startling ease.

Old November Men:
shuffling to the bar,
taking the unlit seat,
muttering masterpieces to the shadows,
and the stout, and the gin and the rum,
with young couples,
laughing heartily with new, moist throats,
deep, full lungs and straight backs,
at our Old November Men,
in yesterday's Sunday Suit.

Old November Men:
switching the light off,
cowering from winter
under the paltry covers,
which seem thinner, too, this weather;
the chill reaches the marrow,
shivers the body and numbs the teeth while
downstairs, the milk has turned sour and the papers stack up.

The highway passes over the lot,
the jets pass over the highway,
and sleep is hard for these Old November Men.

The Liminal Sorts

Around here, we live for the dead.
We share our blood, cells, minds with ghosts
in bell-bottom jeans and corduroy jackets,
we share our throats with the voiceless, the teeming dead,
buried and left in the cool, noiseless earth.

Around here, we listen for the dead.
We follow the pulsing, swelling tides of history,
cock an ear to internal squalls of familial hurts,
toss our sticks into angry rivulets, and watch
as they catch and turn in the eddies.

We cast lots by the pricking of our thumbs,
the warmth of the wind,
the petrichor hanging over the graveyards and
the rhythms of war chants beaten on coffin lids.

One day, I'll go to Omagh and Long Kesh,
the Bogside and Birmingham,
and fill my pockets with the rubble,
so the dead may walk with me.
And the lot of them, the liminal sorts,
lacking their normal insouciance,
will stop on their way to heaven or hell,
cries drifting through the streets
like the burnt scents of funeral tallows:
Your brother is gone, let him lie.
Your sister is gone, let her lie.
Let them all lie and wait, for the rest of us.

IV

Grand Canyon

As you talk.

As I talk.

Echoes fall around us;

a cacophonous reminder

that the gulf in our sensibilities

is immense and cavernous.

Ours is a seismic rift to which tourists
will flock from all states,
and emerge, gawking from sputtering station wagons,
soda-sticky, car-warmed brochure in one pink hand,
trailing, texting, petulant brat in the other.
They, immune to parental chidings,
will leer down unimpressed,
and kick stones down into our grand chasm;
completely ignorant of

how much sheer geological effort,
how much hulking, lithic force,
how much grinding, attritional, tectonic will it takes

to become such vastly different people
in the space of one conversation.

Probably a Bit of Pathetic Fallacy

Heads bowed in penance, we receive our lashings.
Sharing breath, forging rivulets, borrowing goosebumps;
hairs rising like makeshift barricades in meagre defence.

Huddled together, bleating calves in an abattoir,
we hold hailstones in our hands,
feel pockets burn with St. Elmo's Fire,
hear the wind's angry melodies blaring like bomb sirens,
and all the shelters full, and our tongues full, too,
with the haemolytic fear that we will be found,
burnt up beyond recognition,
on someone's front lawn, next to the drenched hydrangeas.

Still, the soaking,
tongue-lashing from an angry grandmother sky,
hammering rain on a skin-tight canvas;
the tumult and the tempest,
reminds me of our worst fights,
and why I didn't want to go camping in the first place.

Easy Love

Anyone can fall in love in a coffee shop.
It takes no great talent, no tremendous force of will.

Anyone can fall in love in the moonlight,
with the internal cinematic orchestra tuned and ready
to pluck and bow and twinkle the heart from *here* to *there*.

Amoebae in the stagnant pool of some Himalayan cave,
could fall in love at the theatre,
with life and death played out before them, and each small movement,
annotated by Shakespeare or Synge.

Anyone could swoon on a Saturday night,
when the evening, pregnant
with potential and purpose,
stretches out before them like a lover already bedded.

Our love, though, is not easy.
Ours is weather-beaten and worn.
Tough as old boots, thin as old rags.
Our love is twelfth-grade-algebra difficult.
It is black tea and toast at Lough Derg,
the second language in your forties,
the last cigarette before Lent,
the last words before heading through security.

Ours takes the sort of Herculean might
that grinds continents together and raises mountains from sea floors.

Your love astounds me.
Mine breaks you.

Gobi

These days, far from the sticky perspiration
and the fruit-flesh tastings of our first season,
I see us fossilizing together.

Nothing too dramatic, of course.

No Vesuvian blankets sweetly stifling our days
and suffocating our worst natures,
no singing, singeing bolide to roar dampening seas
down on flickering, continent-sized libidos,
leaving us spent;
unable to compete with the spectacular morbidity of the cosmos
and the confused looks of small, furry things
staring up at our feet,
wondering what all the commotion is.

Even now, I can feel the minerals seep into our cells,
osteocytes cementing their forever-homes, little by little,
as we Rapunzel-sleep off another day of furniture shopping:
Colonial, Edwardian, or (more likely) hollow, Swedish milestones
hung around creaking necks.

The petrifying groundwater leaches into my dreams
until I can see us clearly—
prostrate in the sands of the Gobi,
and it scares me how comforting it is to know
that they wouldn't find us for millennia, and when they do,
they'll argue about exactly what we were,
or if we really existed at all.

Koi no yokan

The Japanese have a phrase for the premonition of love.
They can taste it in the air, sense the minutest shift of hormonal tides,
pushing and pulling shallows full of dog-paddling heartstrings.
They are attuned to infinitesimal eccentricities of pheromones,
and the hyperactive fawning of grey matter and gametes.

There is no phrase yet, to my knowledge, that describes
the clairvoyance of falling out of love again.

Probably, the Russians have one.

a ceathair

Dead Language

The Irish have plenty of words.
Mostly they mean *cock*, or *vagina*, or *fuck*;
the lapsed-catholic lexicon is lagomorphically populated
with profane adorations of what our parents called sin.

Still, I have found no language to explain
how, from a distance,
Mount Errigal looks like Kilimanjaro,
how, with a bit of blush, in the right light,
the Foyle could pass for the Seine,
the Lagan for the Danube.

How,
by the moon,
in all dead tongues and cadences,
your words could be mistaken for air,
mine for
rain.

Birds of Paradise

I can't fly home for the funeral,
and my mother understands.
I have to teach, and now that he's gone,
the age of pilgrimages is over.

That day, as they lowered him down,
like they would my grandmother a month later,
a student told me that I reminded her
of a bird of paradise,
because I seemed sad, and far from home.

You see, when the Spanish found them,
and sent them back to Madrid as bullion,
boxed up with walnuts and spices,
they wrote stories about the colourful birds that belonged to heaven,
whose feet, Christ-like, would be raised by angels,
before they touched the ground;

who never landed,
never truly landed.

And I wished to God I'd never taught her that,
and that she'd called me something more clichéd;
a bluebird or a nightingale, perhaps.

Anything, but a bird, living in air.
Anything with a home.

Albatross

If there is a bird to know, it would be an albatross.
Now there is someone who understands what it means to leave.

One day I'll catch one as he lands,
takes a breath, turns to go again.
Excuse me, but what does it mean to be an albatross?
He will look at me, surprised:
Haven't you worked that out yet?
Before I can answer,
I really must be going now, he says, politely;
stretches his wings, and is gone again.

Not a bent blade where he landed.
Not a mark to show he belonged
anywhere but on the wind.

I suppose it's just as likely
that we'll be remembered for ourselves,
and not the spaces we leave behind.

The Space between Breaths

There is a moment, before the exhale.
A quiet.
When all the fussing children, red-faced and breathless,
quell their indignant bed-time songs;
the kettle boils, exhausted parents retreat.
The river slows, the traffic lights show no colour,
the signs in shop windows turn over,
the neighborhood dogs wind in their weary circles,
the fireflies cease their evening tristesse
and even the most malicious cat stops scratching at the bedroom door.
In this quiet, before the exhale,
between the heartbeats of the city, the ebbing of its purple blood,
between the stolen gasps that bring
the dogs, children, parents, kettles, rivers,
    lights, shops, fireflies, and mischievous cats,
I miss you.

In the quiet, I am allowed to miss you.

Panic Attack at a Stag Party in Whitefish, Montana

You are far and I am hiding under dusty thoughts,
dressing in sympathetic mists rising groggily from an evening lake.

Acknowledge, if you will, the well-meaning nudges from whitefish,
milling about through the shallows: *just checking in, bud!*

Behind, porch lights hum and bourbon-sugared voices
sing of lust and where to put it.

Here, though, the stillness of the water races the quiet of the night.
and both lose out to my quickening breaths:

In
     one-two-three-four
Hold
     five-four-three-two-one
Out
     one-two-three-fuck-the-Mississippis-four-five-six-seven.

Breathing is arithmetic.

There is arithmetic too, in the respiring tide,
the wingbeats of nighthawks at the surface,
searching for vibrating needles in the dusk;

I think I know them, or at least,
why tonight and why the water.

Challenge Your Self Talk

Sometimes
I
spiral   outwards.

inwards.   **Other**
spiral   times
I

You are at the   of both.
centre
Thumb and forefinger on
my top.

B i l l o w i n g
C e n t r i f u g a l
F o r c e s.

In with the Tide

Of the things that washed upon the shore,
the saddest was a dog we found,
and kept, more faithful than ourselves,
and never bit the hand.

Of the things that washed upon the shore,
the strangest were our wedding vows;
they looked at us, accusatory,
'cross the foggy years.

Of the things that washed upon the shore,
the greatest was the hope we had
that we could still tread water,
and wait for a ship to pass.

Of the things that washed upon the shore,
the largest was the beach itself,
where we had met, and talked, and loved,
and left our little secrets.

Of the things that washed upon the shore,
the oldest was the house we bought,
it's emptier now than when we filled
its walls with ugly songs.

Of the things that washed upon the shore,
the brightest was the ring you took,
it shone like winking pearl-clams,
fed to the gulping blue.

Of the things that washed upon the shore,
the smallest was a baby boy,
who wasn't quite a thing at all,
but quelled the storm, made consecrate
the sand, the surf, the ring, the dog, the house, the wedding vows,
and there he lies upon the shore,
and we lie with him now.

Uncoupling

Wouldn't it be nice to announce it with such sterile detachment?
As if we were strands of DNA; quickly un   zipped,
easily replicated and multiplied
in the holy soup of a polymerase chain reaction.
Near-carbon copies of our mothers, we could be
snipped and sewn into the tired genomic ladder
of some surprised Siberian Mammoth, resting its eyes in a glacier.

Or maybe we were nudged out of orbit?
Pulled from our projected gravitational path by a waning star
imploding billions of light years away.
Some undiscovered supernova
loitering with intent

at the edge

of our solar system,
blending spiral palettes of the galaxy
with ugly blots of colour from our fingertips:
green for my jealousy, blue for your indifference.

It would be nice if we could carefully titrate
the
last
few
dying
months;
the rabble of anxious pentaquarks,
the dull, doormatted neutrons,
even the rowdy, chanting electrons into something of alchemical worth.

Or, at the very least, a more cinematic ending
than a grey Sunday morning,
with neither of us saying much of anything,
and thinking up ways to pretend it wasn't our fault.

Scales

On the
>   balance

of things,

the day I met your dad was probably worse.

I haven't drunk red wine since.

On the
>   balance

of things,

the time we found bed bugs in the moving boxes was more scarring.

I still scratch at my arms when I ride the train.

On the
>   balance

of things,

I was sadder the day my favourite author died.

I hid in the bathroom to read the news, because you hadn't seen me cry
yet.

On the
>   balance

of things,

I probably miss them more too.

On the
>   balance

of things,

I'm sure I prefer my best friend's company.

Which was probably a warning sign, or something.

On the
>   balance

of things,

I know my writing will improve with a broken heart.

Even as we had *the conversation*, I could hear myself trying out lines.

On the
      balance
of things,
I know we were never well suited anyway.
We read each other's favourite books grudgingly, and stopped there.

On the   of things, I know you didn't love him. Not really.
      balance
      balance
On the   of things, I suspect you didn't love me. Not wholly.
On
      the
         balance
           of things,
              the birds will sing tomorrow
              and the world will turn tomorrow,
              and you will still exist and I will still exist, only,
                            on the balance of things,
a little less so.

Epiphanies at the End of the World

Tides have loosed their tongue upon me,
spit vociferous surf upon the shores,
acid that burnt away the sand and
bade the seagulls fly, far as they can.

Mountains have roared raging fires down,
volcanoes wept with pain, and heat,
heat everywhere reigned; the forests, the skies, the seas.

No bricks have been laid for years
and the last tree just tumbled,
creaking agedly to the black soil,
landing like mute dust.

The world's been without song,
birds are memory, and probably always were.
How could such things exist?
Nothing flies, nothing crawls, nothing laughs,
except the dark, which claims greedy inches.

The universe folds back, square by square.
Soon I'll see the horizon approaching,
like a stranger in the wet night long ago,
when a star still hung defiantly in the void,
before it, too, faded.

These things have passed and you are still not here.

Remainder

All that's left
is your morning whispers
and your too-loud laugh at my first-date jokes.

All that's left
is sleep-warmed sheets and Sunday plans;
the warning cough,
before you'd really let me have it.

All that's left
is your throat-caught toneless songs,
the mild nausea of winding ocean roads
and the smell of your rain-soaked, Tuesday-evening-shift jacket.

All that's left
is your morning whispers.

I am beginning to forget.

a cúig

Going Home

When Heaney flew for the first time, and looked down,
he saw his patchwork quilt of greens, nourished by the rain;
a home comfort, something stitched by his grandmother,
passed down with care, for his own children to hold.

Now, flying home again, the prairies without snow seems strange,
makes for the look of an interrupted lover,
caught in some stranger's bed and clutching at slipping sheets,
their canola out for God and everyone to see.

Perhaps, through a window, a white bird in the distance;
it seems so small, but I am small also.

Why, here, no patchwork quilt? he says.

I know this one.

Because this land wasn't made by my grandmother.

He nods, and becomes sky once more.

Being an Albatross

I suppose that's you home for good then? Considering everything.

Yes, considering.

and of course we are in a pub, with warm cheeks,
mouths soft and humming like beehives

and of course home words gently kiss my ears
and whisper not to leave them again

and of course the rain has curled my hair;
holy water drawn from holy roots

and of course the music coming from the parlour
knows me better than God and fills me with Him

and of course I picture a woman in a yellow dress,
who is kind and looks at fish, even strange ones,
as if they were emeralds and
No, I say. *I think I'll be heading back.*

And I finish my drink and leave and think,
I know what it is to be an albatross, after all.

Acknowledgements

THANKS TO EVERYONE at the University of Alberta Press for publishing this book, and treating me so well throughout, particularly Michelle Lobkowicz, who was its first champion, and Cathie Crooks, who answered my many questions about the mysterious world of publishing. Thanks as well to copy editing (and Jimmy Cagney) expert Kimmy Beach for her fantastic work on the book.

Some of these poems have previously found their way into magazines, anthologies, and newspapers. I'd like to thank Matthew Stepanic at *Glass Buffalo* for taking a punt on way more than he should have: "Blood Warm," "Although I Can See Him Still—"(a title borrowed with thanks from Yeats' "The Fisherman"), "The Blazer Brigade," and "At the End of the World." Thanks to Bernard O'Donoghue for commending and printing "Persephone Starts to Wonder" (as "Shoreline Glances") in *Wild Atlantic Words*, Nessa O'Mahony and Jane Clarke at *The North* for taking in "Strange Kettle of Fish," *The Open Ear* for publishing "Hemingway's Cosmonaut," and Black Spring Press for republishing the same poem in *The Best New British and Irish Poets 2019–2021*, Tory Black at *Turf and Grain* for printing "Blue Plain Skies," and Ciaran Carty for publishing "September" and "Sanctuary" as part of the Hennessy New Irish Writing series in *The Irish Times*. I'd also like to thank judge Doyali Islam and the Edmonton Poetry Festival for selecting "Brine" as the winner of the 2020 PoFest Poetry Prize.

My sister, Anna, is always my first editor, and I'd like to thank her for going easy on me and for always looking after me, no matter how far apart we might be. Harry and Ellie were just wee babies when I wrote this so they couldn't lend a hand, but I know they would have done, were they able to. Thanks to my brother-in-law Matt and cousin Andy for the encouragement, and to my grandparents, both here and gone, Hugh, Angela, Esther, and John, for writing so many of these poems with me. I'll never be able to put into words how much my parents, Una and Dominic, have given me. Suffice to say, they gave me enough confidence to go out alone across the Atlantic, and a home I miss so much I wrote a book about it. Mum: thanks for reading everything I write, and everything Terry Pratchett wrote. Dad: thanks for reading *Swallows and Amazons* to us when we were kids, and teaching me patience through suffering with our shared love of Everton.

I am so grateful to all my friends who got me through tough times and were then forced to read many drafts of this book, especially Richard Hyndman who has been with me on the Canadian adventure since the beginning, but *especially* Raven Germain, whose opinion I value so highly. Special thanks to my partner Meghan Dueck for indulging my late-night writing and for being the woman who looks at strange fish as if they were emeralds—I love you. There have been too many wonderful people to mention, but brief thanks in print to Doug Higginson, Greg and Brittany Funston, Christopher Djuric, Tory Black, Paul McIlvenny, Mrs. Pat Rice and Mr. Patrick O'Neill (two very fine English teachers), Susan Kagan, Landry, both Daltons, Michelle, Hallie, Kev, Mick, Julie, Claire, Matt, Kathleen, Ian, Jade, Emma, Anne, Mark, Annette, Sharon and Brian Graham, Sharon and *Bryon* Steinke, Irv, Denise, Burnsy, Steph Blais, Scott, Blake, Danielle, Jess, Rylan, Steph Guin, Mark Devlin, the whole paleo gang with Phil and Eva...and particular thanks to Cody Steinke for sharing his home, the art of the bit, and thousands of hours of films with me.

Finally, if you've picked this book up because of the title, a last one, for you:

Sometimes, a Haiku

you will muddle through

love moves on with reluctance

friends will always help